Mummies, Tombs, and the Afterlife

Elspeth Graham

PACIFIC
L E A R N I N G

© 2004 **Pacific Learning**
© 2001 Written by **Elspeth Graham**
Photography: The Art Archive: pp. 5, 12 (right), 13 (middle), 14; British Museum: p. 7 (top), Corbis/Archivo Iconografico, S.A.: p. 20; Corbis/Asian Art & Archaeology: pp. 15 (top & bottom); Corbis/Bettman: p. 6 (top right); Corbis/Jeremy Horner: p. 21; Corbis/Hulton Deutsch: p. 11 (bottom); Corbis/Charles & Josette Lenars: pp. 4, 7 (bottom right), 8, 10; Corbis/Craig Lovell: p. 11 (top); Corbis/Dennis Marsico: p. 22 (top left); Corbis/Roger Ressmeyer: p. 6 (bottom); Corbis/David Samuel Robbins: p. 22 (bottom); Corbis/Kevin Schafer: p. 23; Corbis/Vanni Archive: p. 13 (top); Corbis/Adam Woolfit: p. 19 (middle); Corel Professional Photos: Title Page; Michael Holford: p. 12 (top & bottom left); Sîan May: p. 22 (top right); Science Photo Library/John Daugherty: p. 6 (top left); South American Pictures/Tony Morrison: p. 9; Werner Forman Archive/Viking Ship Museum, Bygdoy: p.19 (bottom); Werner Forman Archive/Egyptian Museum, Cairo: p. 13 (left & bottom right); Werner Forman Archive/Silkeborg Museum, Denmark: p. 7 (bottom left).
Front Cover: Werner Forman & Martin McKenna.
Back Cover: Corbis/Charles & Josette Lenars
Illustrations are by Jeff Anderson, Stefan Chabluk, Antonia Enthoven, Nicki Palin, and Martin McKenna
U.S. edit by **Alison Auch**

This Americanized Edition of *Mummies, Tombs, and the Afterlife*, originally published in England in 2001, is published by arrangement with Oxford University Press.

08 07 06 05 04
10 9 8 7 6 5 4 3 2 1

Published by
Pacific Learning
P.O. Box 2723
Huntington Beach, CA 92647-0723
www.pacificlearning.com

ISBN: 1-59055-377-2
PL-7319

Printed in China.

Contents

Introduction

Most ancient peoples believed in life after death. Death was seen as the beginning of another life – the afterlife – so preparations for death were very important. These preparations, or **rituals**, helped dying people and their families to accept death. Death rituals varied from one ancient **culture** to another.

People of many cultures believed that they would need their bodies in the next world. One way to **preserve** a body after death was to mummify it.

▲ A South American mummy bundle

Many ancient peoples left everyday objects beside dead bodies. They thought these things would be useful in the afterlife. For some people, seeds and a digging stick were important. For others, tools and pots were essential, or perhaps a sword mattered most.

Royalty and rich people were often buried with gold and amazing treasures. These **grave** items inform us about the way these ancient people lived.

Dead bodies were often put in special places, such as caves, graves, **tombs**, or **burial chambers**. Sometimes, bodies were placed together in cemeteries.

▲ An Egyptian mummy mask

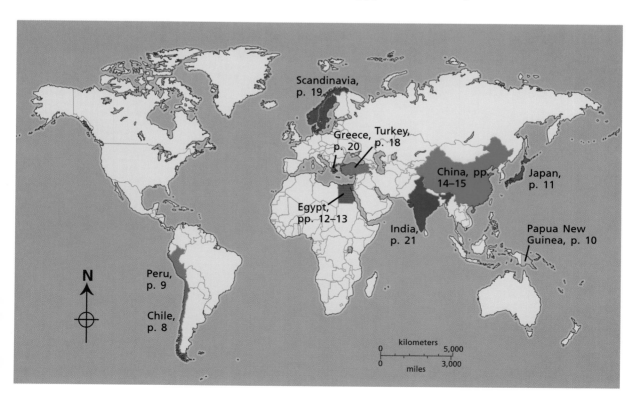

Scandinavia, p. 19

Greece, p. 20

Turkey, p. 18

China, pp. 14–15

Japan, p. 11

Egypt, pp. 12–13

India, p. 21

Papua New Guinea, p. 10

Peru, p. 9

Chile, p. 8

N

kilometers
0   5,000
0   3,000
miles

What Is a Mummy?

A mummy is a dead body that has been preserved. It still has some soft tissue (skin, muscles, or organs). The tissue makes it different from a skeleton. A skeleton has no soft tissue; only the bones remain.

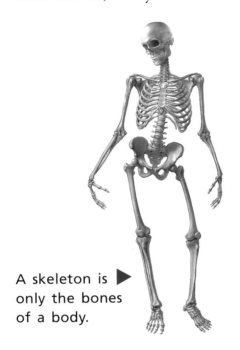

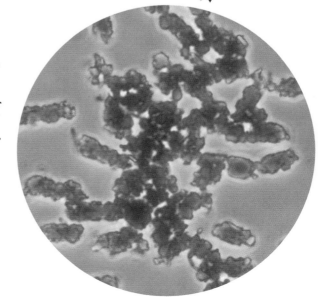

◄ A mummy has some soft tissue.

A skeleton is ► only the bones of a body.

Bacteria ▼

After death, a body normally **decays**. If decay can be stopped, a body can be preserved. Decay is caused by the action of tiny living things called bacteria. Bacteria cannot live without water, air, or in freezing temperatures. Most mummies were created by drying out the body in the sun, or with chemicals, fire, or smoke.

Accidental Mummies

Sometimes people have died in places where natural conditions halted decay. Accidentally mummified bodies have been discovered in caves, bogs, deserts, and frozen in ice.

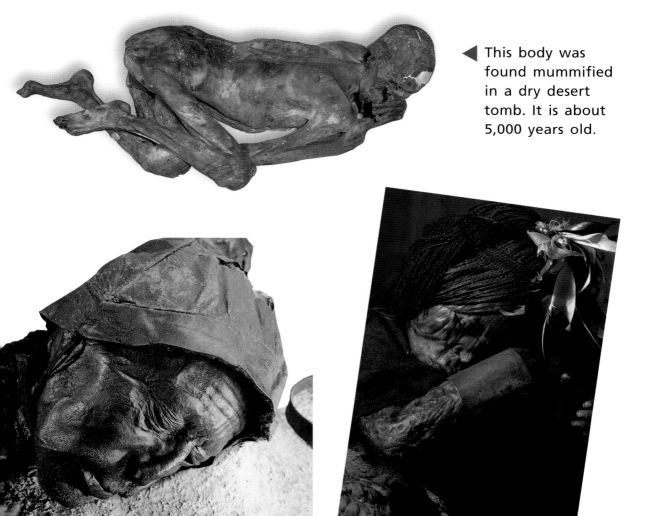

◀ This body was found mummified in a dry desert tomb. It is about 5,000 years old.

▲ Tollund Man was preserved in a Danish bog for about 2,000 years.

▲ This mummy was frozen 500 years ago in the highest mountains in Chile.

The First Mummies

South America

The Chinchorro

The Chinchorro people were making mummies 7,000 years ago. These are probably the oldest mummies in the world. The Chinchorro lived in one of the driest deserts on Earth.

SOUTH AMERICA

PERU

Paracas

Inca

Chinchorro

CHILE

▲ A Chinchorro mummy could have looked like this.

They took apart the bodies of the dead and dried out the pieces. Next, they tied sticks to the bones to reinforce the bodies, and then they put the pieces back together again. The Chinchorro then covered the bodies with paste and painted them black. Finally, they painted on faces.

The Chinchorro mummies were found in cemeteries.

The Paracas

The Paracas people wrapped cloths around their mummies. Gold, food, clothing, weapons, pots, and even pet animals have been found tucked inside the cloth layers.

See Mummies on Display, page 10

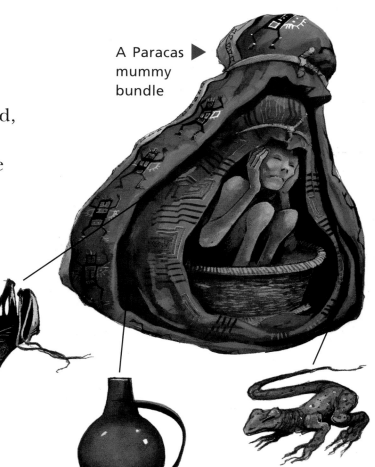

A Paracas mummy bundle

The Inca

The royal mummies of the Incas were worshipped as gods. They were seated on thrones in tombs and had servants to take care of them and bring them food.

The mummies of ordinary people were buried in large cemeteries and were tended to by the old men. Land was even set aside to grow crops to feed the dead.

▲ An Incan tomb

Mummies on Display

Not all ancient peoples kept their mummies in tombs or graves. Some mummies were treated as part of the household, or put out on display, or even worshipped.

See The Incas, page 9

This drawing from 1600 shows a royal Inca mummy being taken on parade. ▶

Papua New Guinea

In Papua New Guinea, dead bodies were hung in smoke to mummify them. The Papuans were proud of their mummified **ancestors** and displayed them in places of honor. Mummies were brought into the house where the family's new possessions were exhibited for them.

PAPUA NEW GUINEA

▲

Honoring a mummified ancestor in Papua New Guinea

Japan

Most Japanese mummies were once **Buddhist** priests. A priest who chose to become a mummy would go on a starvation diet. No one really knows if starvation helped to mummify the bodies because, like the Papuan mummies, Japanese mummies were also hung in smoke to dry. Many Japanese mummies were painted and displayed in temples. Some are still worshipped.

See Egypt, page 12

▲
A Japanese Buddhist temple

JAPAN

FACT **BOX**

Mummies have also been thought of as curiosities. Egyptian mummies were put on display in museums and in private homes. In the nineteenth century, they were even unwrapped on stage as entertainment!

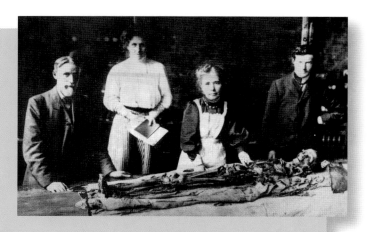

Masters of Mummification

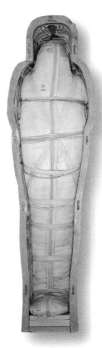

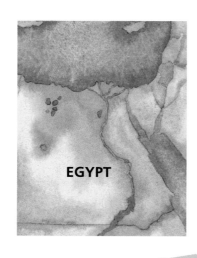

EGYPT

Egypt

The ancient Egyptians believed that the **spirits** of the dead needed bodies as well as a tomb to return to. Egyptians became accomplished mummy makers.

How the Egyptians Preserved Bodies

◆ The body was laid on a table.

◆ A hook was pushed up one nostril to remove the brain.

◆ The major organs, except the heart, were taken out and put into jars.

◆ The body was rinsed with wine and packed in salt.

◆ After the body was dried, oil, sweet-smelling herbs, and spices were rubbed into the skin.

◆ The body was padded.

◆ Makeup was painted on.

◆ Finally, linen cloths wrapped the body from head to foot.

The organs were put into canopic jars
▼

▲
An Egyptian **sarcophagus**

Amazing Tombs

Egypt

Everything an ancient Egyptian might require in the afterlife was crammed into the tomb. The largest of all the tombs were the pyramids of the **Pharaohs**.

◄ The Great Pyramid is the world's largest stone structure.

▲

Cobra and bracelet from a tomb

King Tutankhamen

Unlike the pyramids, the tomb of King Tutankhamen had never been robbed, and its dazzling treasures were discovered in 1922.

See Grave Robbers, pages 16–17

FACT BOX

When a mummy was carried into a tomb, the "Opening of the Mouth" ritual was performed. A priest touched its eyes, ears, mouth, and jaws. This meant the mummy would be able to see, hear, speak, and eat in the afterlife.

King Tutankhamen's death mask ▶

China

Like the Egyptians, the Chinese filled their tombs with extraordinary treasures for the afterlife.

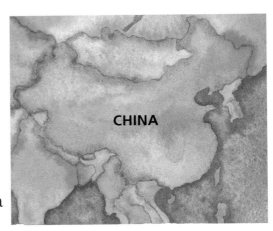

CHINA

Emperor Qin Shi Huangdi

For example, Emperor Qin Shi Huangdi surrounded his tomb with a buried army to protect him in the next world.

◀ In addition to life-size horses and chariots, more than 6,000 **terra-cotta** soldiers were discovered guarding Qin Shi Huangdi's tomb.

FACT BOX

Qin Shi Huangdi's tomb has not been **excavated** yet. Legend says that inside there are rivers made of mercury, gold and silver ducks, trees of **jade**, and jewels like stars.

Princess Dou Wan

The Chinese believed that jade could preserve bodies. Unfortunately, it did not work. The Princess Dou Wan had a burial suit fashioned out of jade. When her tomb was opened, though, it was found that her body had turned to dust.

Princess Dou Wan's jade burial suit ▼

Lady Dai

In contrast, Lady Dai's coffin contained the most perfectly preserved mummy ever found, in addition to breathtaking riches.

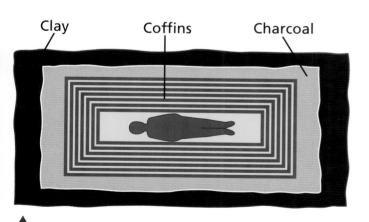

Clay   Coffins   Charcoal

▲
Lady Dai's tomb was surrounded by charcoal and thick layers of clay that kept out air and moisture.

◀ A painted banner from Lady Dai's tomb

15

Grave Robbers

Everyone knew that tombs and graves were full of valuable treasures, especially the magnificent tombs of rulers and wealthy people.

See Emperor Qin Shi Huangdi, page 14

- The Chinese ruler, Qin Shi Huangdi, killed everyone who worked on his tomb so that its dazzling secrets would be kept safe.

See King Tutankhamen, page 13

- The pharaohs built false doors, hidden entrances, networks of passages, and many other traps into their pyramids to try to trick robbers. Yet by 3,000 years ago, every pyramid had been entered and robbed. The pharaohs stopped building pyramids. They built concealed tombs deep within rock cliffs instead, but the robbers still got in.

- In the Middle Ages, a book called *The Book of Buried Pearls* told people how to break into tombs and pyramids. It also provided magic spells to protect thieves from evil ghosts.

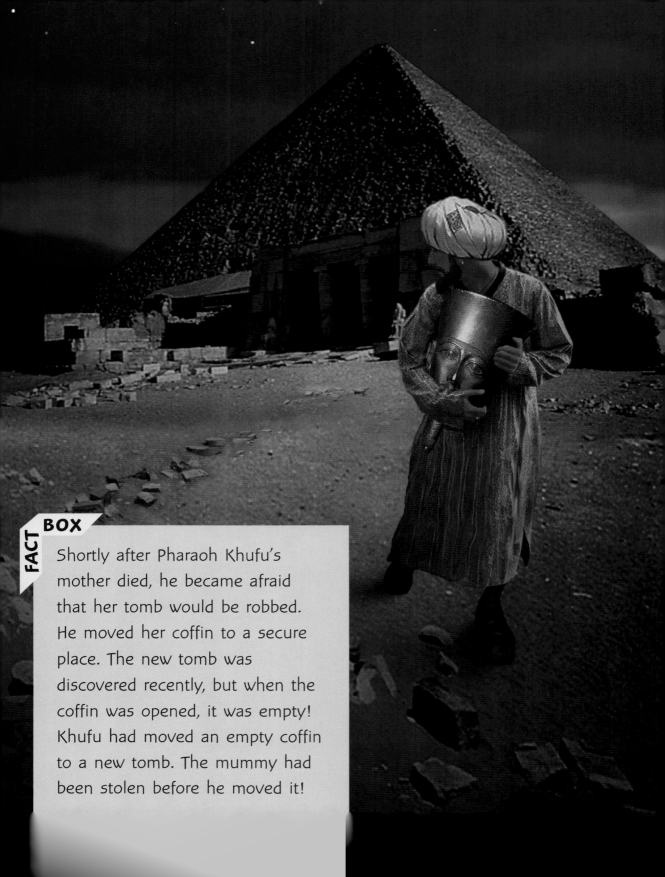

Beds of Bones

Turkey

Nine thousand years ago, the people of Catal Huyuk in Turkey did not preserve the bodies of their dead relatives or build tombs for them. Instead, residents put bodies on high platforms outside the **settlement** and left them there.

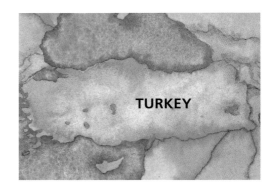

TURKEY

When the bones had been picked clean by vultures and other birds and insects, they were collected and put under platforms in the family homes. The platforms were used to sit on during the day and to sleep on at night.

Journeying to the Afterlife

Scandinavia

A dead Viking would be put into his ship, with all his possessions, to journey into the afterlife. The whole ship would then either be set on fire or buried under huge mounds of dirt.

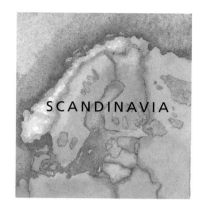

SCANDINAVIA

A few Viking burial ships have been excavated. Not only did they contain the remains of human bodies, the ships were also packed with clothes, weapons, furniture, cooking pots, and jewelry. Horses, cattle, dogs, and even servants were killed and put on the ships, too.

A carved dragon head 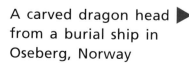 from a burial ship in Oseberg, Norway

Greece

The ancient Greeks believed that a dead person's spirit would depart from the body and travel to the underworld. They believed the underworld existed deep underground. To get there, the dead had to be rowed across the black waters of the River Styx by Charon, the ferryman. The dead were buried with coins to pay Charon.

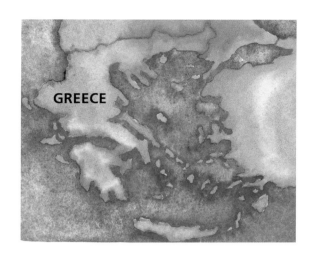

GREECE

▲
A sixteenth-century painting by Joachim Patinir showing Charon crossing the River Styx

India

Hindu people believe that when a dead body is **cremated**, the spirit is freed and can then live again in another body. This is called reincarnation.

For many centuries, Hindus in India have come to the banks of the **sacred** Ganges River to die. The ashes from the funeral **pyres** are gathered and scattered in the river.

▲

In the city of Benares, the Ganges is lined with "ghats" (steps) that lead down to the water. Some have platforms on which the dead are cremated.

21

Modern-day Memorials

People have always had rituals to help them accept the death of family and friends. Today, most people bury or cremate dead bodies. Very few mummies are made anymore. Still, all around the world people mark burial places with **memorials** to honor and remember people who have died.

Respect for the Dead

Ancient peoples treated their dead with care and respect. Everything possible was done to make the journey to the afterlife as easy as possible.

Mummies and their burial places hold many clues about life in the past. We learn a tremendous amount about how ancient peoples lived from the everyday objects and treasures found in tombs.

Ancient graves and tombs are still being found and excavated. Yet, despite the fact that the ancient dead and their belongings are now treated with more respect than they once were, many people believe that their burial places should be left undisturbed.

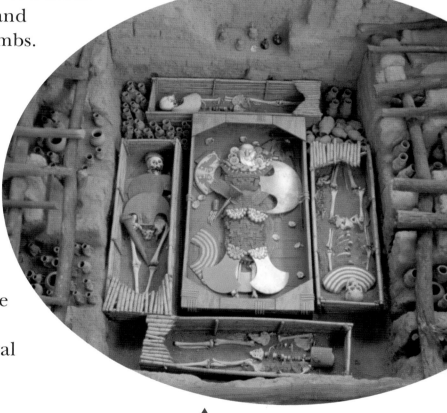

▲ A warrior's tomb in Peru

Glossary

ancestor – a member of the family who lived a long time ago

Buddhist – a person who follows the teachings of the Buddha

burial chamber – a cave or room where a dead body is placed

cremate – to burn a dead body so that only ashes remain

culture – beliefs, goals, and practices of a group of people

decay – to break down into tiny parts

excavate – to uncover by digging carefully

grave – the place where a dead body is buried in the ground

jade – a semiprecious green gemstone

memorial – something used to celebrate or honor a memory

pharaoh – a ruler of ancient Egypt

preserve – to prevent decay

pyre – a pile of flammable material for burning a dead body

ritual – a set of movements or actions

sacred – holy; special in a religious way

sarcophagus – a stone coffin

settlement – a small group of houses

spirit – the part of a person that some people believe never dies

terra-cotta – a reddish brown pottery

tomb – a place, sometimes a chamber, where a dead body is buried

Index